WEEKLY WR READER®
EARLY LEARNING LIBRARY

Staying Safe
At Home

by Joanne Mattern

Reading consultant: Susan Nations, M.Ed.,
author/literacy coach/consultant in literacy development

Please visit our web site at: www.garethstevens.com
For a free color catalog describing Weekly Reader® Early Learning Library's list
of high-quality books, call 1-877-445-5824 (USA) or 1-800-387-3178 (Canada).
Weekly Reader® Early Learning Library's fax: (414) 336-0164.

Library of Congress Cataloging-in-Publication Data

Mattern, Joanne, 1963-
    Staying safe at home / by Joanne Mattern.
        p. cm. — (Safety first)
    Includes bibliographical references and index.
    ISBN-13: 978-0-8368-7791-5 (lib. bdg.)
    ISBN-13: 978-0-8368-7798-4 (softcover)
    1. Home accidents—Prevention—Juvenile literature.   2. Children's accidents—Prevention—
Juvenile literature.   3. Safety education—Juvenile literature.   I. Title.
    HQ770.7.M332   2007
    613.6083—dc22   2006030333

This edition first published in 2007 by
Weekly Reader® Early Learning Library
A Member of the WRC Media Family of Companies
330 West Olive Street, Suite 100
Milwaukee, WI 53212 USA

Managing editor: Valerie J. Weber
Editor: Barbara Kiely Miller
Art direction: Tammy West
Cover design and page layout: Charlie Dahl
Picture research: Diane Laska-Swanke
Photographer: Jack Long

The publisher thanks Brittany and Kathy Bohlman for their assistance with this book.

Printed in the United States of America

1 2 3 4 5 6 7 8 9 10 10 09 08 07 06

Note to Educators and Parents

Reading is such an exciting adventure for young children! They are beginning to integrate their oral language skills with written language. To encourage children along the path to early literacy, books must be colorful, engaging, and interesting; they should invite the young reader to explore both the print and the pictures.

The *Safety First* series is designed to help young readers review basic safety rules, learn new vocabulary, and strengthen their reading comprehension. In simple, easy-to-read language, each book teaches children to stay safe in an everyday situation such as at home, at school, or in the outside world.

Each book is specially designed to support the young reader in the reading process. The familiar topics are appealing to young children and invite them to read — and reread — again and again. The full-color photographs and enhanced text further support the student during the reading process.

In addition to serving as wonderful picture books in schools, libraries, homes, and other places where children learn to love reading, these books are specifically intended to be read within an instructional guided reading group. This small group setting allows beginning readers to work with a fluent adult model as they make meaning from the text. After children develop fluency with the text and content, the book can be read independently. Children and adults alike will find these books supportive, engaging, and fun!

— Susan Nations, M.Ed., author, literacy coach,
and consultant in literacy development

Home is a fun place to be!
Do you know how to be safe
at home, too?

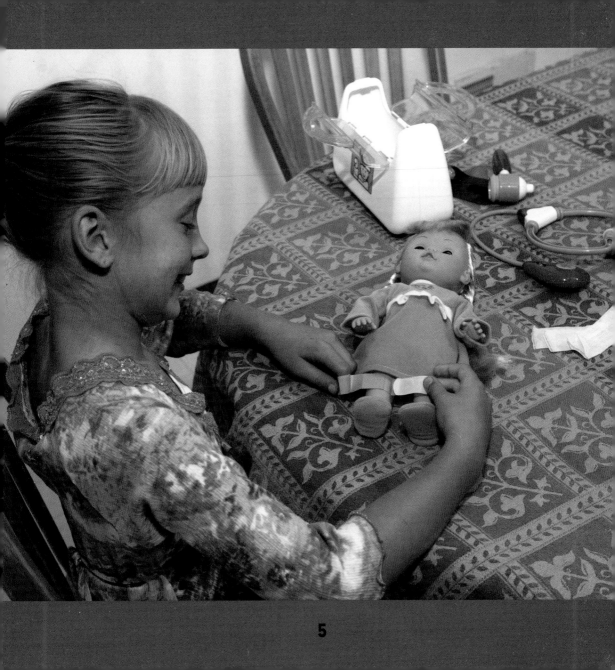

Some things can make you sick. The wrong **medicines** can hurt you. Stay away from cleaning **supplies**, too.

cleaning supplies

You should never use a sharp knife. Ask a grown-up to cut up food.

The stove can burn you. Ask an adult to heat food for you.

Every home should have smoke **detectors**. Their **buzzers** warn you when there is a fire.

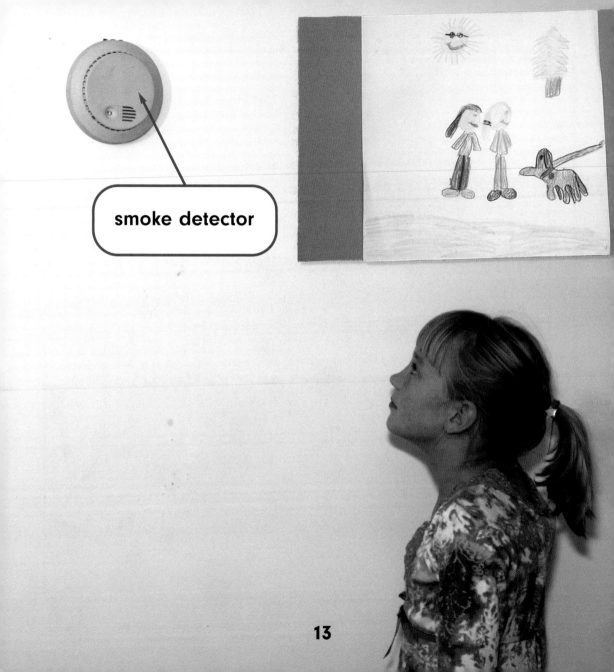

smoke detector

13

How would you get outside if there was danger? Plan how to **escape** from each room. Then **practice** with your family!

Never play with matches or a gun. Both can hurt you or others.

matches

What would you do if someone is badly hurt? Call 911! The **operator** will send help.

Mom 555-2143
Dad 555-8822
Grandma 555-6143
Help 9-1-1

19

Know your address and telephone number. Help keep your family safe, too!

440

address

Glossary

buzzers — electric machines that make buzzing noises. They give a signal about something.

detectors — machines that warn of something

escape — to get away

medicines — drugs taken for a sickness

operator — someone whose job it is to answer the telephone

practice — to repeat something many times to get better at it

supplies — items used to do something

For More Information

Books

Do You Smell Smoke?: A Story About Safety with Fire. Hero Club (Safety) (series). Cindy Leaney (Rourke Publishing)

Home Fire Drills. Fire Safety (series). Lucia Raatma (Bridgestone Books)

Home Sweet Home: A Story About Safety at Home. Hero Club (Safety) (series). Cindy Leaney (Rourke Publishing)

Watch Out! At Home. Watch Out! Books (series). Claire Llewellyn (Barron's Educational Series)

Web Sites

Code Red Rover
www.coderedrover.org
Learn how to stay safe with a family emergency plan and more.

U.S. Fire Administration for Kids
www.usfa.fema.gov/kids
This fire safety site for kids includes puzzles and games.

Publisher's note to educators and parents: Our editors have carefully reviewed these Web sites to ensure that they are suitable for children. Many Web sites change frequently, however, and we cannot guarantee that a site's future contents will continue to meet our high standards of quality and educational value. Be advised that children should be closely supervised whenever they access the Internet.

Index

About the Author

Joanne Mattern has written more than 150 books for children. She has written about weird animals, sports, world cities, dinosaurs, and many other subjects. Joanne also works in her local library. She lives in New York State with her husband, three daughters, and assorted pets. She enjoys animals, music, going to baseball games, reading, and visiting schools to talk about her books.